SOME TIMES I TELL THIS TALE TO THE RIVER

To Imroz, Osho, and Sai

SOME TIMES I TELL THIS TALE TO THE RIVER

Amrita Pritam

Translated from Punjabi by

Arlene Zide

HIND POCKET BOOKS

SOME TIME I TELL THIS TALE TO THE RIVER

Cover design and illustrations: Imroz
First paperback edition, 1996
ISBN 81-216-0516-4

Published by
Hind Pocket Books (P) Ltd.
18-19, Dilshad Garden, G.T. Road
Delhi-110 095

Designing, Typesetting & Print Production :

SCANSET

18-19, Dilshad Garden, G.T., Road, Delhi-110 095
Tel: 228 2467, 229 7792, 93, 94 Fax: 228 2332

Printed at Vikas Offset, Delhi-110032

PRINTED IN INDIA

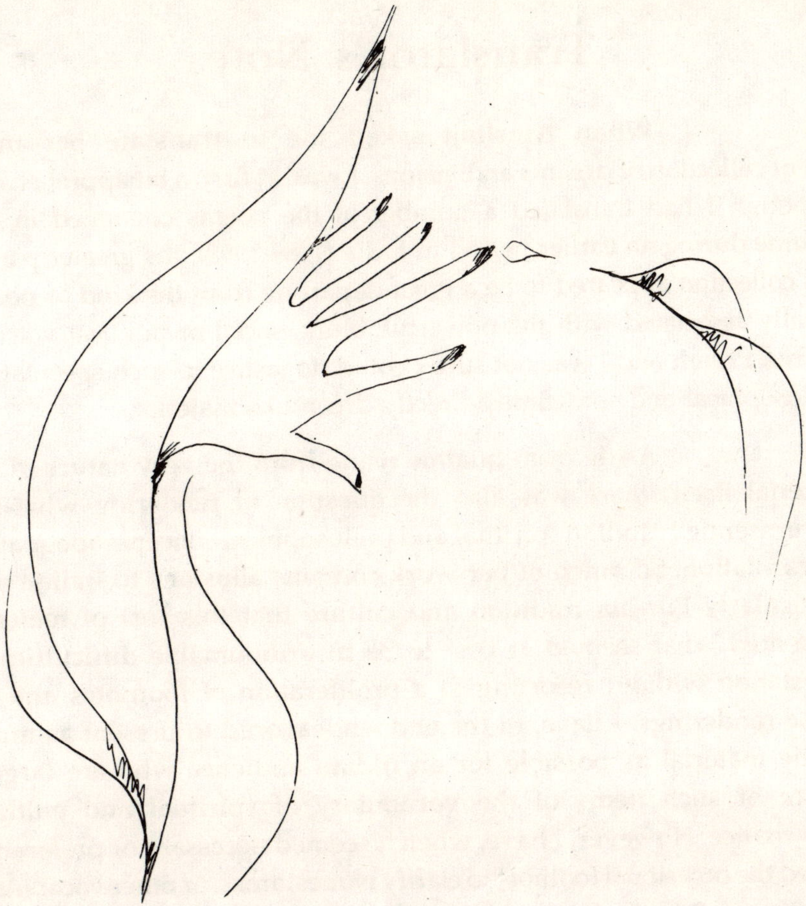

Translator's Note

When Amritaji asked me to translate her more recent collection of dreams and visions, I was, at first, a bit apprehensive. Although I had translated a number of the poems contained in this volume during an earlier period in India (1989-1990), the greater part of this collection appeared to be a great departure from the kind of poetry usually associated with the powerful, blunt, social or political voice of Amrita Pritam and I was not sure I could do justice to such speculative, philosophical and sometimes directly dreamlike material.

Aside from qualms rising from the very nature of the material itself, there was also the question of rendering what are quintessentially Indian spiritual and philosophical concepts adequately in translation. So much of her work contains allusions to Indian and particularly Punjabi tradition and culture that this sort of material presented what seemed at first to be insurmountable difficulties in translation without resorting to a proliferation of footnotes and/or prose renderings. I have, in the end endeavored to present as much of the material as possible for an Indian audience who are largely aware of such items of the vocabulary of spiritual and cultural provenance. However, I have, when it seemed necessary or preferable, added the occasional footnote to clarify names, areas, or other vocabulary peculiar to Punjab or otherwise less likely to be known.

Although not often, in a number of instances, liberties of transcreation have been taken in order to bring across the essence and ideas behind the literal words; this, always in consultation and collaboration with the poet herself. So that, for example, in *Desert Lila*, where we have in Punjabi, *dachi*, a female camel, with romantic associations, we have varied the words/concepts as e.g., dromedary, or the metaphoric 'ship of the desert' etc., so that the rather more prosaic and epicene 'camel' of English does not lose the flavor of mystery in the original Punjabi poem.

In a number of the poems, the original Punjabi contains rhyme, slant rhyme, and deliberate rhythmic repetitions which are the music of the Punjabi words. While it has been impossible to recreate this consistently in the English, I have, wherever I could do so, attempted to use inverted syntax or other means to reproduce some semblance of the rhythmic lilt and rhyme in the original. Attention thus has been paid to recreating the sound-look of the Punjabi insofar as this has been possible, and it is hoped a genuine sense of the original has thereby been preserved.

New Delhi, 1995 *Arlene R. K. Zide*

Surrounded By Lions

Many, many years ago an incident occurred which even today is shrouded in mist for me. I was very young. In Lahore, in our Chunamandi house, there was a very large room where my father sat — with very old manuscripts spread all around him. He called some scribes in to copy a few pages of manuscript.

One day, I went into the room, without wearing anything on my head, and my father slapped me. His orders were that whoever came into that room had to cover their head. To his mind, this was a mark of respect for the books. At that moment, I tolerated that slap silently; but I felt that as much as I tried to forget it, I couldn't do so. After a few hours, I was running a high fever.

My mother came and put cool compresses on my forehead; I looked into my mother's face and said: "He slapped me just because of these books; well, I can write such books myself! And I know that I've written them!" Even today I don't know how such fated words came to my lips.

It happened on the 11th of December, 1985; I came across a book that I had written in a past life. I saw an open book. I started reading whatever was in front of me and a shiver ran down my spine. In the dream, I called to Imroz: "Look, this is a book I wrote in my past birth."

I read two paragraphs of the book, and I read one out to Imroz and then I woke up. Some lines I remembered, but I regretted that I had forgotten the other paragraph and did not know the title of the book. The following are the lines I did remember :

She felt
that in the corner of her heart
there was a wall of stones
from where the ayats[1]
of the Quran appear

Today, when I look back at my earlier years, I can see that this chain of dreams began when I was very young. On one occasion, there was a dream I had at a very early age that I can still see clearly. All around was a jungle and I was standing there alone when five lions roared.

I just knew they were going to eat me and when they were very near I said to them: "I have to write a poem; please let me write it first; then, you can eat me."

---

[1] *ayats — stanzas of the Quran (Koran), like slokas.*

The lions smiled and gave me a sheet of paper and a pen. I searched for a place where I could sit and write. In the distance I saw a stream over which a house which looked like a bridge had been built. Showing the house to the lions I asked: "May I go inside the house and sit there alone to write?"

The lions agreed and I went into the house and could see that the lions had surrounded the house. The house was empty. I closed all the doors from inside so that the lions couldn't get in. I peered out through the crack in the window and saw that they were standing there, surrounding the house.

I felt reassured that they wouldn't be able to get in through any door, but at the same time I was worried that I would die of hunger and thirst inside. And then I saw that there were some small steps on the floor of the house leading to the river. I could go down these steps into the river and drink

But there was another worry — I could get water, but how would I assuage my hunger? Then I saw that there was a room full of fruit — there was so much fruit that I would be able to eat for many days. And then I calmed down till another thought came to me — when there was no more fruit, then what?

Then I saw that the other room of the house was full of dried fruits and nuts. There were so many that one could spend one's whole life there and not finish them.

To this day, I cannot fully fathom this that nature revealed to me at such an early age; and for years, I didn't really understand. These days, however, I think that the chain of events is continuing but now I discern a difference.

Now, when something happens, and the same question arises in my mind, I think I find the answer from within. However, sometimes, a voice answers me. I cannot recognize the person whose voice it is usually, but sometimes I can see the person. Though I cannot recognize him, he comes and gives me the answer.

Maybe those five lions were the symbols of the five elements of which my body is composed, or may be of something else, I still do not know. But since then I can see a dog or a bear smiling at me in the same way. Sometimes not only smiling, but also talking to me.

I have seen some statues smiling too — statues of Ganeshji and Shiva. And once a Shiva statue lit a lamp in his hand; and once, he spoke and told me the secret of my death in a past birth.

But I can now say that the very first dream of the five lions which nature showed me set the pattern of my life. There will always be danger around, but I will manage to get food and peace of mind from within.

– Amrita Pritam

Why call it dreams,

Why not say "a being in contact with realities in another dimension?"

— *Homage to the Sun*

Fate

It was at an early age that I met Sahir. One night, I had a dream that he and I were in a boat, and there was water all around on four sides. We couldn't see the shore we'd left and we couldn't see the shore towards which the boat was headed.

Then I heard a voice: "This is your fate." I recognized the voice even in this dream. It was my father's.

When I woke up, my eyes were full of tears. After that, I had to go through so many years to write many poems so full of agony.

Even throughout my life, I could see water everywhere, the water which had lost both shores. I realized that perhaps this was the meaning of fate. God knows how many poems I have written, whose letters trembled in my hands.

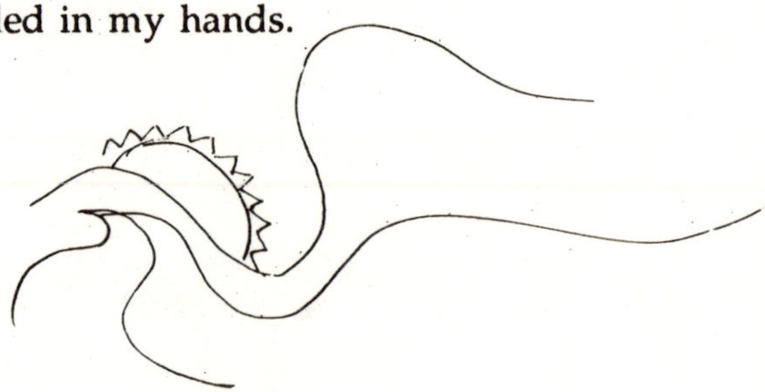

Early Spring

The gypsy of spring came,
a bundle over his shoulder.
People stood there watching in amazement
as I bought the musk of love.

What a blessing — this purchase of mine!
Those who laughed at me yesterday
have come begging for a pinch of that musk today.

The suffering of love is the precious mortar
where, like kohl, I ground my life.
It is every evening that the sky
descends, and begs from me,
a needle's worth for his eyes.

In the water of my two eyes
I stirred my dreams.
Today, the earth has entered my courtyard
to color her dupatta.

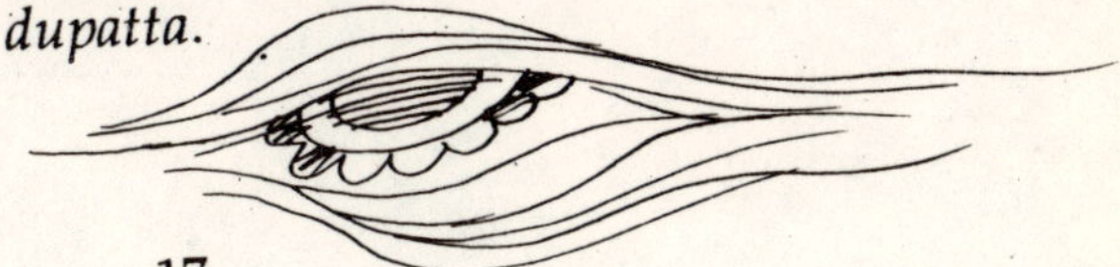

My hut is made of stalks.
My life, a seat of reeds.
Like a guest, today,
the spark of your memory
has entered my house.

My fire is a blessing to me;
The sun came to my doorstep today
and asked for an ember
to kindle his own fire.

My Friend, Oh, My Stranger

You came once, suddenly.
Absolutely astonished, Time
stood motionless in my room
the sun was about to set
but could not,
and for a little while forgot its fate.

The cosmic order complained,
a quizzical look upon his face,
looked at the moment
and jumped quickly from the window.

Remembering this incident I wondered
and you wondered too
And perhaps, Time
cannot afford to repeat this mistake again.

Now, every day the sun sets on time
and darkness descends within me every day.

Now, you and I may admit it or not
but that incident in the past was the truth.
And that day, when he jumped from the window
Time bruised his knees and bled.

Beneath my window sill
that stain of blood lies frozen still.

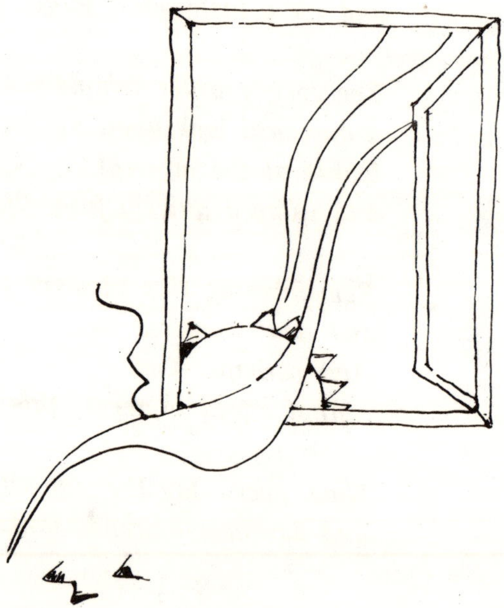

A Meeting

We met suddenly, after several years
We both shivered like a poem.

The whole night before us
but half the poem stayed in one corner
and the other half
in the other corner.

We met at daybreak
like torn pieces of a sheet of paper.
I grasped his hand in mine
He clasped me in his arms.

Then again, like censors
we both laughed.
We put that sheet of paper on the cold table
and crossed out the entire poem.

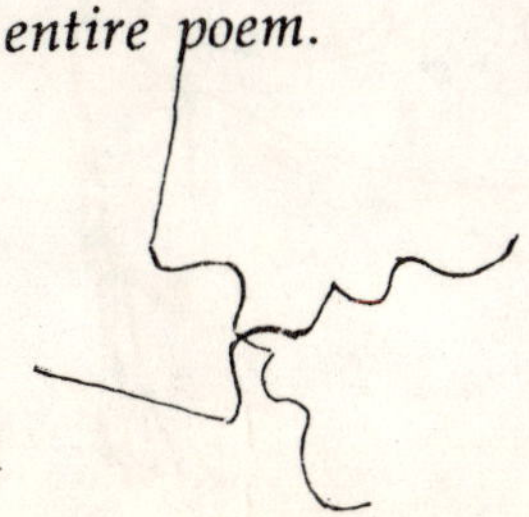

The Desert

In the desert I saw a small hut which was mine; I was standing next to it and looking around. Except for the sand, I could not see anything.

What I know is that I had the feeling that someone was lost out there. And in the dream, I realized that there was a sound of steps coming from somewhere; in the dream I said to myself: "Look, my Life, don't close the door. Listen, there's a sound of steps coming from somewhere." Then, when I met Imroz in life, I felt it was an invitation from the unknown.

"Now I have to go to the unknown."

The Sigh That Breathes Fire

Today, the sun was puzzled,
Opened a window of light,
Closed a window of clouds
and descended the stairs of darkness.

There was a sheen of perspiration
on the eyebrows of the sky,
I don't know why.
Shedding his moon-shirt,
he undid the stars.

Now I sit here in a corner of my being.
A memory of you came
like the thick and bitter smoke
that rises from damp wood.

With it came so many thoughts—
the way parched wood breathes out
its crimson sighs of flame.

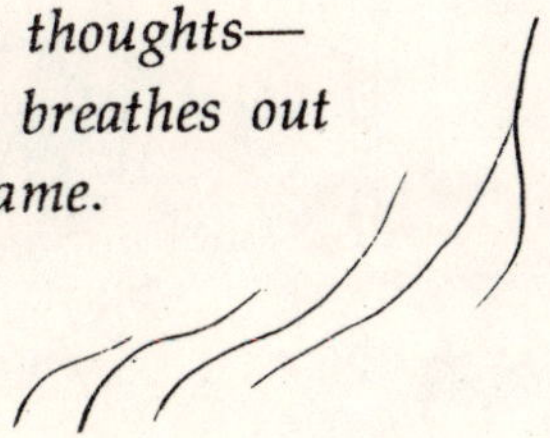

I have put out both those fires.
The years of my life are like scattered coals
Some have gone out, some smoulder still.
The hand of Time began to sweep them aside
and he blistered his fingertips.

From the hands of your love
I this earthen vessel fell, and was broken,
History came to my kitchen today,
but went away hungry.

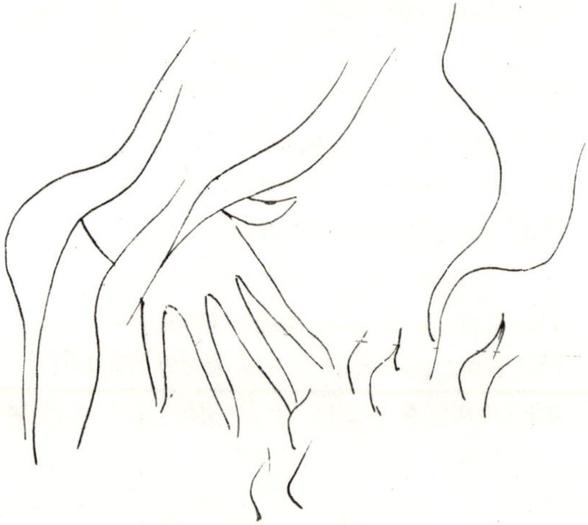

Winter

My being shivers,
lips have turned blue,
A tremor has arisen from the feet of my soul.

On the sky of my age
the clouds of the years are thundering
In the courtyard, hailstones of the law rain down.

If you come today,
passing through the mire of the alleyways
I'll wash your feet,
your sunlike body.
Lifting the corner of my blanket,
I'll warm my bones.

I'll down a cupful of sunlight in a single gulp
keep a fragment of that sunlight in my womb
and then, perhaps I'll live out the winter of my life.

The Bridge

Yesterday, we burnt the bridge
separating our destinies like two banks of a river.

Our bodies started when we saw
the wasteland of one body on one bank,
the wasteland of the other on the other bank.

When the seasons brought us flowers
You tore them from your body
I too returned, to the seasons
and the many years, like fallen leaves,
— we threw them in the river.

Years have passed
but the rivers haven't dried.
And in their flowing waters we have
seen our shadows
though not each other really.
Before our lives,

standing at a distance, end
let us spread our withered bodies
over the body of the river

You walk on your own body and cross
one half of the river
and I will walk now on my own, meeting you
halfway.

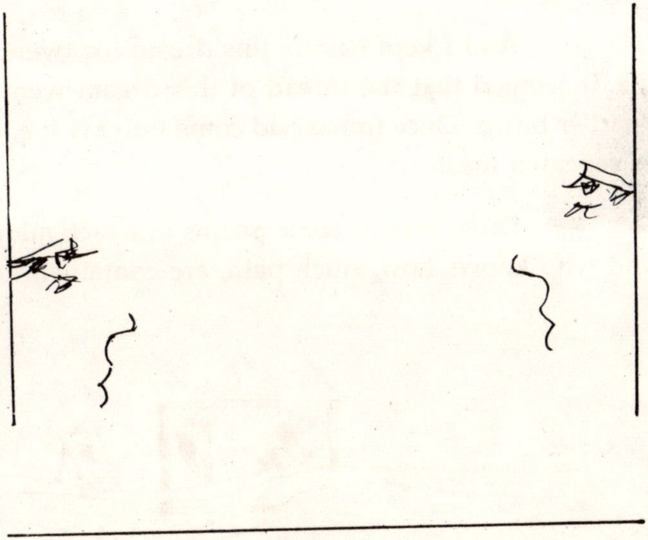

A Twenty-Year Long Dream

Somewhere where there was no *bustee* around, I could see a house. And on the upper floor, I could see a window; through it could be seen a stream and many trees outside.

Often I would see someone standing at the window; but from behind, I could see that he had a warm shawl over his shoulders. Sometimes he would be sitting next to the window and sometimes he would be painting.

And I kept having this dream for twenty years. After a while, it seemed that the thread of this dream went far back into some earlier births. Once Imroz had come into my life, this dream no longer repeated itself.

Later, I wrote some poems in which many years of my life, and who knows how much pain, are contained.

Invitation

The woman, Night, was celebrating,
The stars like rice in her winnowing fan
Who will prepare a feast of them?
Who has brought the crescent wine jar of the moon?
The eyes of the sky are heavy with drink.

The heart of the earth is throbbing
I've heard that the flowers have come as guests
to the branches of the trees.

What will happen later on?
Who will go and ask Destiny?

On the scroll of my life
Your love has put its thumb print
Who will keep the accounts?
Destiny has written a song.
I am told someone will sing
that very song tonight.

Beneath the shade of the kalap tree
Kamdhenu is overflowing with milk
Who can fill the pots?
Who cares for the sighing of the wind.

Let me go. Destiny has come for me ...

Kalap tree — a mythological wish-fulfilling tree
Kamdhenu — the mythological cow whose milk flows endlessly

Blasphemy

Today, I have sold a world
and bought a world of beliefs.
I committed an act of blasphemy
I wove a bolt of dreams
tore off a yard
and sewed a blouse for my life.
Today, I took off a lid of clouds
from the earthen water-pot of the sky.
and sipped its light from my palm

I will pay with my songs
for these moments
I have borrowed from death.

Phoenix

On the one hand, there was the partition of the country and the violence that I saw in the name of religion. Those dark forces shook the roots of the values I grew up with. On the other hand, my personal opposition took many shapes.

Every other day, yellow journalism made its living spreading some rumor or another. And many times, there were those who raised their voices to ban my poems and stories.

This nightmare did not last for just a few days, but went on for years. Then, one night I found myself in the form of a phoenix. I dreamt of a jungle full of flowers; and there a phoenix sat on a tree singing, as if its voice had been filled with agony. Flames were coming from its wings. When the flames rose higher, I saw the phoenix burning in them.

This was the dream, but that was when I realized that it was I who was the phoenix. I saw myself burning and then turning to ashes.

When I awoke I wrote some poems; and then some time later I wrote a long poem, *Words*. Every line contains events as if they were part of my autobiography.

It is said that the phoenix is born from its own ashes. This must be true, since I've watched myself being reborn many times out of my own ashes.

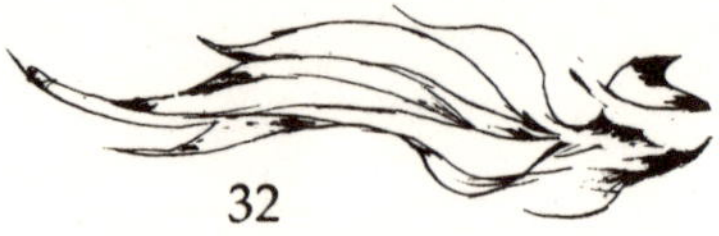

Words

There was a city of stones,
the stones of the dynasty of the sun
and the stones of the dynasty of the moon
and people lived in that city —
it was a kingdom of tyrants
The kings had no ears
and the people no voice,
so that when people wept
they turned to stone.
Stone gods, stone priests
loving kinship never flowered,
the stony silence never came to an end
The sun-horse whinnied loudly,
and pawed at the stones.
The cloud-elephant trumpeted
and uprooted the stones.
The darkness of the night hissed,
coiled like a snake on the stones
And then the decree came down—

Section one-forty-four.[1]
The stones sat cowering
in the corner of their own hearts
Then, like some deep desire from within
a pale leaf or flower, or some blade of green grass
grew from the stone like tapasya
— his meditation broken,
the rishi shuddered.

Life flickered off and on
and so in this city of stone
a stone dynasty burgeoned.

A flat slab and a round stone were, in that city,
destined to meet
and both tasted the forbidden fruit.

Now sometimes the thought comes to me ...
If I were a green leaf,
a sigh of their bodies, or a delicate tendril
Then, their breast would have been my fortune.

---

[1] *Section 144 : During the British Raj, when voices were raised for independence, the colonial government issued decree 144 which forbade more than five people to walk together down the street; there were no trials for those accused of violating the decree; people could be shot outright if accused.*

The sun-horse kept on whinnying
and the cloud-elephants kept on trumpeting
and the serpents of the night kept on hissing out
the tyrant's decree.
But I could have sat at ease in the shelter of the stones
and hidden myself in the crevices of their tenderness.

But perhaps they were made of flint
that under the dirty sky
and on the dirty earth
slept on a bed of stones,
and rubbing these stones together, I was born
like a spark in the season of fire.

When the fire was born
the stone shuddered and the slab shuddered, too.
They took the fire into their laps
and gave it its first taste of smoke
The midwife wind laughed and laughed, but
the mother, who had given birth, just wept.
"Fire cannot play in the laps of stones
The sorrows of stone have no end.
On the tongues of stones even blisters are stone.

We belong to the earth and you to the wind."
Then, absolute silence.
They said nothing more
and before they closed their eyes
they probably didn't notice
the newborn fire heave its sigh of flame.

On the lips of fire a long sigh is written
and in the bones of fire there is only smoke
Wherever these blowing winds carried me
the hot ash of my body sifted down
and whatever day came into my life
I embraced it and it turned to ashes.
I felt — does the line of my fate waver
like the line of the smoke?
Is the fire of the funeral pyre born
from the wombs of mothers?
I was burning like the funeral fire.
Sometimes in the darkness of sleep
I could see a blue flame of dreams
and I felt that the fire of the funeral pyre
was an insult to the fire.

The fire within a Sassi, a Sohni, a Hir—[2]
I felt I knew that fire
The funeral pyre is not the only fire
that is an insult to the fire
and it seemed that in the city of stones
those fires lit by Waris[3]
were my inheritance.
Only fire can inherit fire
But no one can kindle fire in a city of stones
Nobody warms their hands on the fire of the mind
And on my tongue
there erupted a blister of fire.

They who belong to the city of stones
kept on saying — Put out this fire
Hide it in some cellar
Keep it hidden
very deep within!

---

2 *Women from various love legends of Punjab. Sassi died in the desert, Sohni drowned in a river, and Hir was poisoned*

3 *Waris Shah, the most famous poet of Punjab, wrote the love epic of Hir and Ranjha, still sung in all of Punjab today*

Into her gullet stick your thumbs in deep!
Throw her into the racing river!

There was a city of stone on a shore of stones
Nobody shared the agony of the fire
The wind that took me in her lap, who gave birth
to the mother of the mother of my mother
She came
running from somewhere
bearing some words in her palms
"Don't think of these little black things as lines
This handful of lines
are the allies of the fire
Look — words have the spirit of fire
and the spirit of fire is greater than fire itself."

Saying this, she rushed on ahead.

May the life of your fire
be found in your words.

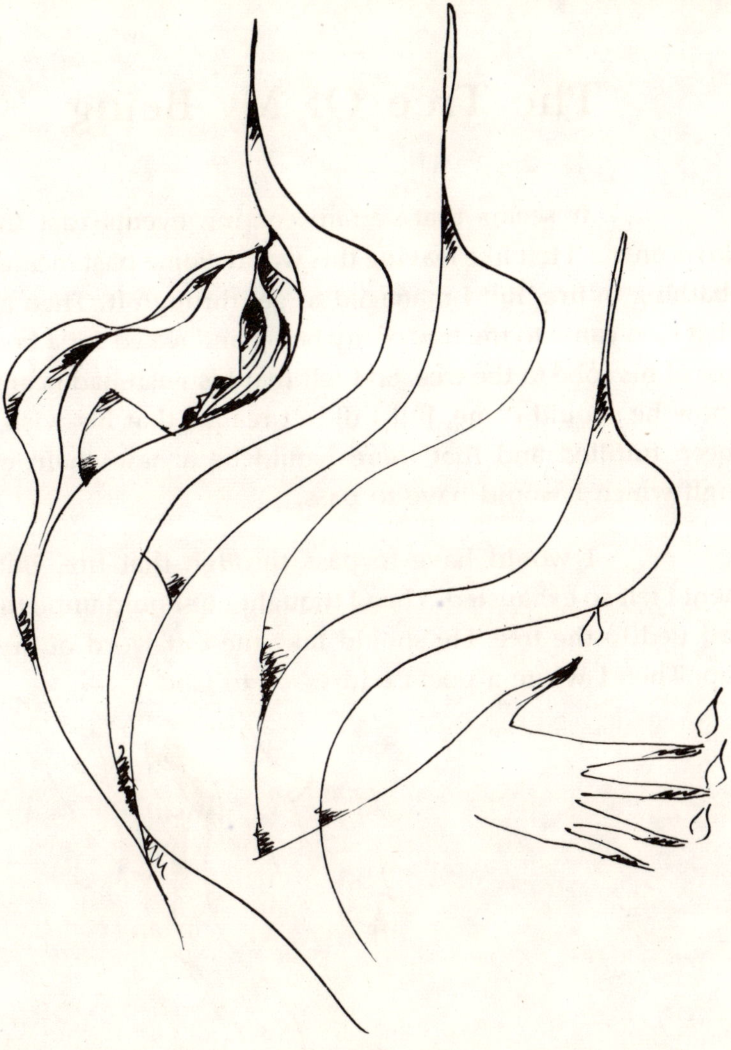

The Tree Of My Being

It seems that certain coming events cast their dark shadows on me. I felt like leaving this world. Some past incidents were like bathing in fire. But I managed to get through it. Then one day I felt that God came to the tree of my being and asked for a boon, tying a piece of his robe to the tree. So I felt that his wish had been fulfilled and now he should come. But I didn't realize that his wish had not yet been fulfilled and that there would be a new chain of events through which I would have to pass.

I would have to pass through that fire. But at that moment I felt so exhausted. Then I thought he should untie the thread he had tied to the tree. He should take the last word of my soul in his lap. Then I wrote a poem addressed to God.

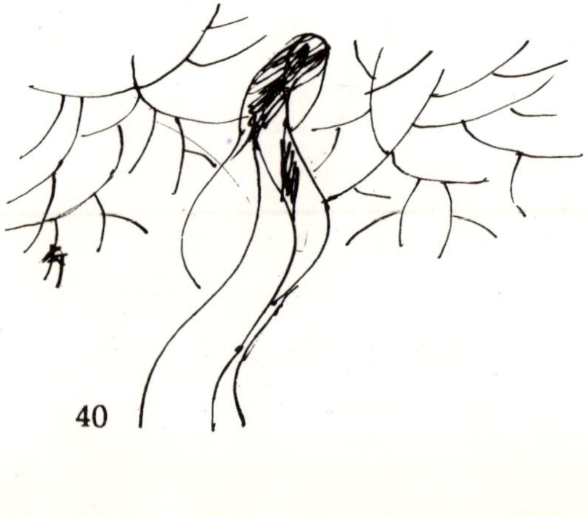

O God

God, you
Came to this tree that is me
one day to beg a wish,
tore off a piece of your robe
and tied it to this tree.

Each and every drop of my blood
I turned into each and every word I wrote
And those very words of mine
were strangled by the world.
I saved the honor of my birth,
I never wept,
because you came to me, God,
and asked for a wish.

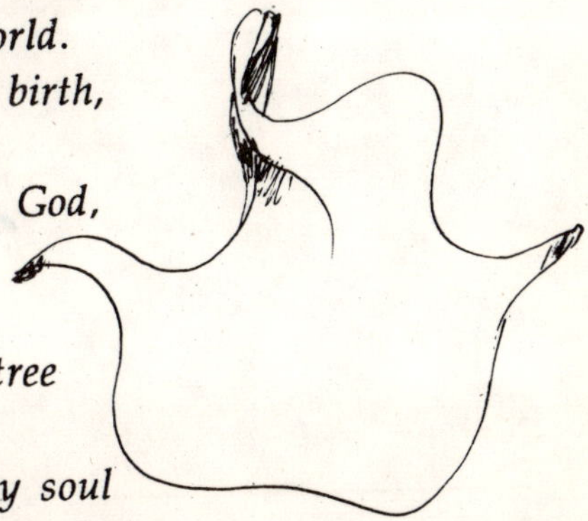

Now, God, come to the tree
and untie the strip.
And this last word of my soul
take it in the folds of your robe.

God, once you came to this tree that is me
and made a wish.
The wish you wanted
has been fulfilled

There is a custom of going to a shrine-tree such as a Pipal *and tying a strip of cloth on its branches to ask for a wish. The strip is untied when the wish has been fulfilled.*

A Journey

What I saw is still before my eyes. In some wilderness there were some ruins through which I was walking. I peered at every stone as if ...

Sometimes I feel that these are the remains of some palace, and somewhere I feel there was a monastery in ancient times, and it is one of this monastery's broken walls that I recognize.

It seemed that at some time life was pulsating there and I realized that these were some throbbing moments which, standing there, had turned into stones. Then I had a dream within this dream, and remembered what I had just seen, and I was writing a poem.

In that dream I touched the moss on some stones and when I had written almost half the poem, I woke up and felt that the wet moss still clung to my fingers and feet. And I found myself rubbing my feet as though they were still wet.

The half of the poem that I wrote in the dream, I set down on paper; and completed the other half of the poem when I woke.

August, 1987.

A Journey

Last night I went to the ruins of my subconscious mind
and watched some instances of time.
Perhaps they hovered, whimpering, in the air
their feet frozen in sorrow;
and then, for a long time
perhaps their shadows quivered,
stuck, like moss to the backs of stones
lying on the ground.

To one side lay the broken tower of a palace,
and to the other, the broken monastery wall.
Touching the moss on the stone with my fingers
first, it laughed
and then, it wept.

Oh God—
What happened?
What kind of consciousness is this
that returned from those ruins?

My legs and feet ached
as if they had been on a journey of many births
and breathless, I had walked for many ages.
And now, I can see that moss
falling to dust from my fingertips.

A Fleeting Glimpse

It was much later when I witnessed a vision of cosmic power. But there had been many glimpses of it for many years. And a fleeting glimpse of my own birth — that I was born to a woman who was serving a great *Rishi.* And there was a young disciple who loved my mother, but couldn't express his love because she belonged to the guru. And that was the reason the young disciple's meditations were disturbed. Then, after centuries, he became my father in this birth.

I don't know how many threads of how many births are not known to me but there were some that had snapped and then been rewoven into my being.

And in this cloudy state of mind, I wrote the poem, *Darshak: I Am Witness to That Moment.*

Darshak:
I Am Witness To That Moment

I am witness to that moment
when suddenly, an idea came to a ray of the sun,
when I brushed away the cosmic dust
and accepted the dust of the fields.
I am witness to that moment.

And when a speck of that dust
went in search of another speck
and chose a womb of flesh
filling it with a spark.
I am witness to that moment.

When a constellation smiled
and analyzed what sort of seed it was,
I am witness to that moment.

This was the passion of that speck
but when it took the form of a deep sigh

heaving itself from my chest
I accepted it with respect
as a tilak on my forehead.

I am witness to that moment.

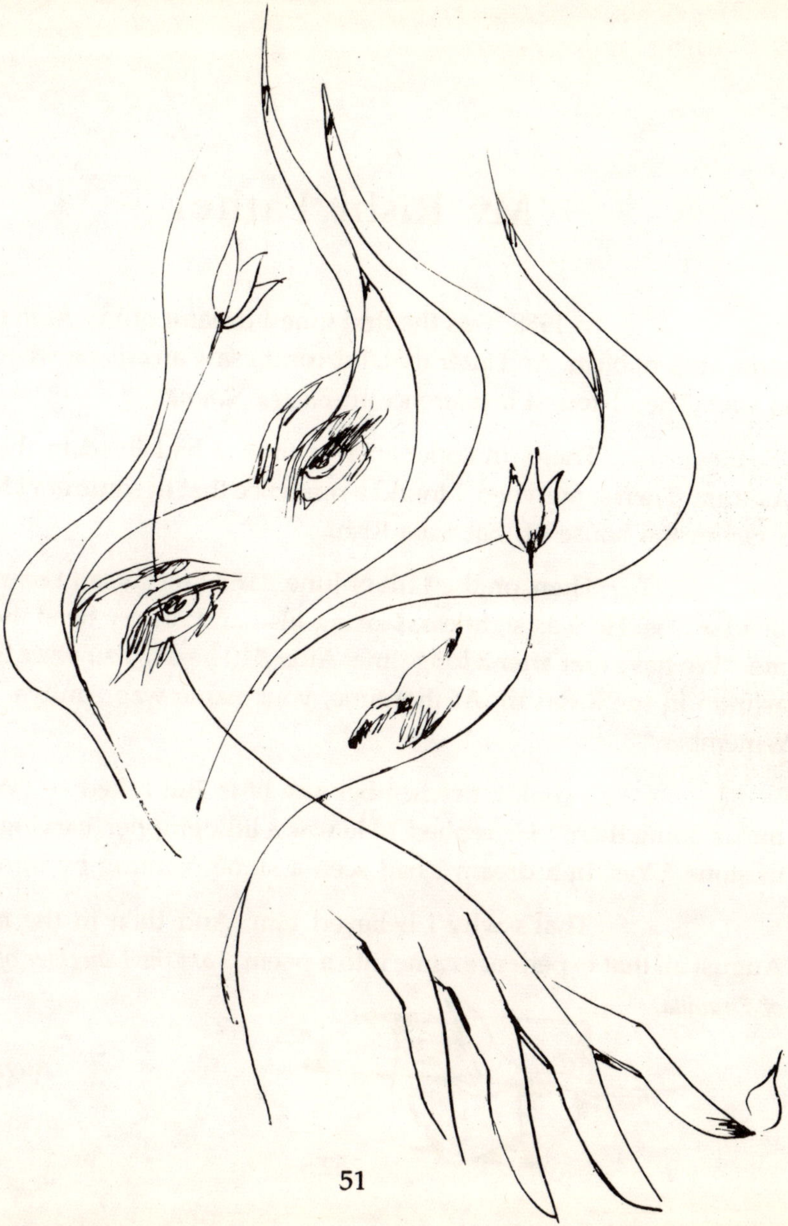

My Rishi Father

In 1988, was the first time I dreamt of my *Rishi* father in some ancient birth. And after that, I dreamt I saw an *ashram* where I used to stay. Then I found a reference in *Bhrigu Sahinta.*

There, in some ancient time, I had lived in the Bhrigu Ashram. Then somewhere I found a reference that in some era I had been a girl in the house of Jhabwala Rishi.

Then, on the 11th of June, 1988 I met a saint named Ram Bhadar Das. He was sightless. Placing his hand on my head, he said to me: "We have met after a long time. After 510 years. You were in a Rishi ashram in the Rasavali. At that time, your name was Amitya. Try and remember."

I couldn't remember any of it. But asked — "What was Imroz doing then?" He replied, "He was a lithographer, carving pictures in stone." Yes, in a dream I had seen a stone painting by Imroz.

That's why I believed him. And then in the month of August all that experience came into a poem, *I am the Daughter of the Land of Dravida.*

August, 1988.

I Am The Daughter Of The Land Of Dravida

I am Kama-kanya, the daughter of love.
I am Kal-kanya, the daughter of death.
Wearing this body, I have come.
I am the daughter of the land of Dravida.

One by one, I passed
through each of the four ages
and was turned into a mere subject
I am the daughter of the land of Dravida.

Temple, palace, brothel, slum
the allure of the body's clay
The body resides in all of these.
I am the daughter of the land of Dravida.

*The red veil of honor**
The black veil of disgrace
Both colors have fluttered in the air
This was my body's earthly stage
when I wore both colors
and then discarded them
I have merged myself in the depths of my own being.

I am the daughter of the land of Dravida.

* *Red is the color of the marriage veil, considered auspicious.*

Meeting A Rishi

It was the 18th of April, 1988. It was almost morning when a *rishi* appeared in a dream. There was some paper in my hand and placing it before him, I said: "Please look — there Saturn and Venus are sitting together with the sun in the sun's house; what will they do to me?"

At the same time, two bedsteads appeared out of nowhere, on which Venus and Saturn were sitting draped in white cloth. The rishi causally looked at the paper and said, "Yes, you will spend your life under their influence, but what you have to see is that you'll live either deep within you, or else in fear of them."

At that time, while reading my poem, *O God,* which I wrote in 1994 to the rishi, I awoke.

Everything faded away.

But that was the dream which walked alongside me like a shadow. And after two years, I wrote a poem, *The Tree of Silence,* which is a reflection of the dream.

The Tree of Silence

No, I have not picked the words
from the tree of silence
I have gathered up the words
that have fallen from the tree.

No, I have said nothing
to you, or to anyone.
I have just listened
to those words which were speaking in my blood.

There was a streak of lightning
which passed through my breast.
These are the fragments of that streak
that I have counted out upon my fingers.

On a spinning wheel
the moon has spun the clouds.
These are her very same threads
which I have woven on my loom.

No, from the tree of silence
I have not picked the words.

The Dark Forces

One cannot imagine the dark forces in the form of a human being, but one night I witnessed this. I don't know where it was, but there were many people, some sitting and some standing, walking here and there, meeting others. Suddenly, I saw her, in front of me, covered in black clothes, looking like a skeleton. In her eyes was a look that was very frightening and I saw her coming towards me.

She came so close and my whole body shrank in fear. Suddenly, someone came and pushed her back.

Then I saw from a distance that she was surrounded by people; but with what a poisonous look she was watching me! The poison was oozing out of her body. Some dirty-looking white stuff was growing and increasing and it was coming towards me.

Having shown me all this, perhaps nature didn't feel like showing me more. I woke up. I awoke with the deep realization that if I wanted to see God in every little thing, then I must see all this as an observer.

This is the feeling from which I wrote a poem — *She*, in which there is a touch of *Karuna* (compassion.)

She

She was a night
no longer speaking with the moon
when some fire glittered on the forehead of the stars
Feeding them the milk from her breasts
she flicked the stars away
Asking every storm and whirlwind
to be a witness
She was a night,
no longer speaking with the moon

She was a being
no longer speaking with her soul
when the noise burst from her breast
She strewed hot lava on the paper
and hung the paper on the wall
asking the dust of the crossroads
to be a witness
She was a being
no longer speaking with her soul

She was an image of God
no longer speaking with God
when her body of flesh cried out
for her withered now-dead beauty
She decorated her coffin
and covered it with a golden cloth
Then, she asked the pyre on the cremation ground
to be a witness
She was the image of God
no longer speaking with God.

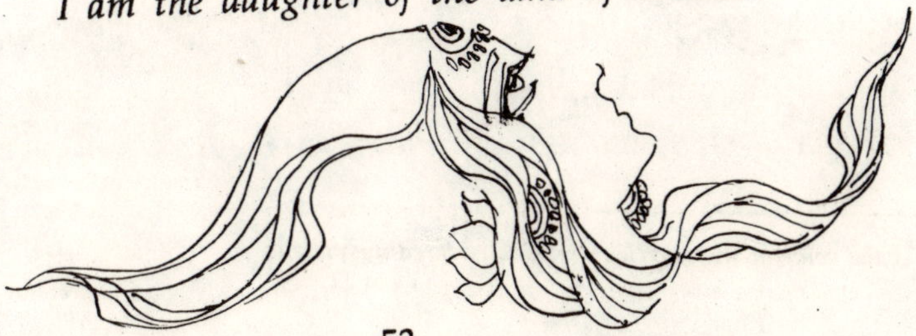

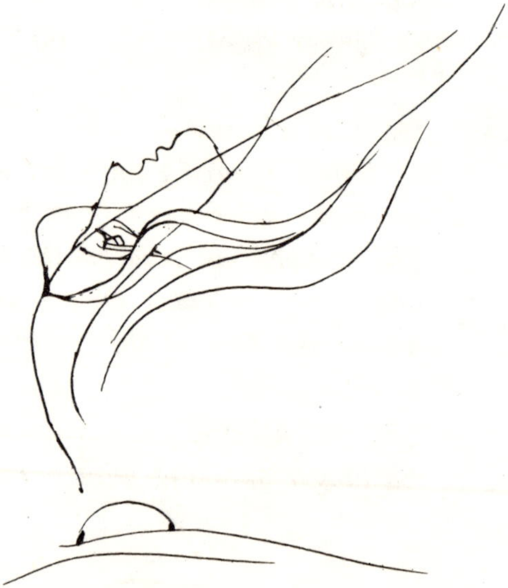

perhaps wanting to tell her something
using his fingers
to write something in the sand...
Then like a whirlwind
a shadow fell
swooping down on her —
sweeping her from the ship of the desert...
The camel shook her neck
and a bell cried out...
Out of nowhere, some protecting shadow appeared
spreading its arms
and steadying her.

You, rider
the breeze whispered into her ear:
These are the memories of many past births
bound up in the bells.

This desert lila will free them
but this wild camel in the desert
will wear you out!

Don't just come into the desert like this,
The wind whispered in her ears:
First, you must go up into the high
mountains
and burn the lamp of your inner being
and worship your pir.
Then the pir will offer your camel
sandalwood and sky-Ganges water,
and then tame her with his own hands.

There was a ray of consciousness
that touched her.
Then, walking in the sands of her own being
she climbed its path.

There was a fragrance coming
from the mountain
telling her of the pir.
Then, she saw the camel
following slowly behind her.

Sai Darshan

It was becoming night when in a lonely place, suddenly, someone came to me and said: "Sai Baba is calling you." I looked towards him in surprise, not recognizing him when he came and asked: "Which Sai? Shirdi Sai? He doesn't know me, so has he himself called and asked for me?"

He nodded yes and a mad feeling ran through my whole body. The stranger indicated a direction and I ran that way quickly. There was a rather dark place where Sai was seated on the ground. I greeted him silently. When I came nearer, he raised his head and looked at me, and asked — "Why are you so sad?"

I stood absolutely still in front of him, and answered:

"Sai, what can I do? There are lies all around me everywhere I turn." This was the only question and the only answer. Then the dream was over.

This happened in 1992 in the early hours of the 14th of March. When I woke, I was astonished, but happy. And for almost a year, I was under the spell of this question—that Sai had been concerned with my well-being.

Almost a year passed, and in 1993, one day I was lighting some incense in front of Sai Baba when I sensed that I was not the one holding the stick of incense, but had myself become the incense. The incense that wanted to burn at the shrine of Sai. And this whole experience came to life, word by word, and set itself down on the paper.

Chillum

Sai, please give me a little bit of fire
from your chillum...
I am your incense
and for a little while will burn
at your shrine.

I have kneaded your passion
into my own clay.
When this body smolders,
smoke will rise.
This body's smoke will flicker
and will say only this much —
whatever breezes pass through —
these touch your breath
I want to become one with those breezes.

Sai, please give me a little bit of fire
from your chillum...
I am your incense
and for a little while will burn

at your shrine
No, I won't say anything.
When the incense burns
a delicate fragrance will say something in a whisper
and then my body
turning to ashes,
will touch your feet.
It must become one
with the earth of your shrine.

Sai, please give me a little bit of fire
from your chillum...
I am your incense
and for a little while will burn
at your shrine.

An Ashram

In 1994, in the month of July, there was a night when an *ashram* appeared before my eyes in a dream. At an earlier time, I had seen some *ashrams*, but this time I knew that this *ashram* belonged to Sai. And I realized also that I was staying there. I saw some other people there but was unable to recognize them.

When I woke, my senses told me that in this birth Sai had no *ashram*. He had sat under a tree for years. Then, he stayed in the ruins of a *masjid*. What I'd seen must have been from an earlier life.

Some days passed till the night of 30th July, when Sai appeared in a dream and said: "Yes, there was an *Ashram*. Its name was *Svet Ketu*. That was 256 years ago."

This was the dream in which I could glimpse that *ashram* even while awake. Where was it? I couldn't find out but I could see it. This obsession flowed in my veins. This state of madness was burning in my veins, and then this sensation of burning found itself in my words.

Ali

Hidden from view behind the hills
a stream was flowing
I would go and bring water
to your shrine from that stream

That day it was the same water
and like every day, I filled your bowl
setting it by your meditation place.

I don't know when it happened
but this much I know—
late that evening
feeling very thirsty, I took a sip
from that bowl.
The same one I had set there by your place,

As if I'd taken a sip of fire.
The night was very cold.
But a burning current streamed through my veins
Restless, I sat outside in the open air

When the reddish glow of the sunrise came
I went to the stream
Sensing something in its breast
waves broke on the surface of the stream
but taking control of the torrent, she said:
Don't ask me about this,
Ask the bowl.
Come and tell me
whatever the bowl says!

Sai, when all the people had emptied out of your shrine
I sat myself down alone near the bowl, trembling.
The bowl laughed and said —
Madwoman!, there are some things that should not
be asked about
You, who deserve this, this sip of fire
Simply take it within you
This is the greatness of Sai
Keep it in your veins.

Sai, I don't know in which cycle of time this happened
but this much I know —

Whatever happened, it happened at your shrine
and I know
when such things happen
they are beyond time
And look —
after passing beyond many deaths
that sip of fire still lives in my body.

Cave Story

In a state of madness, I didn't know if Sai's *ashram* was within me or I in his *ashram*.

In my memory, every twig around Sai's shrine was blooming and I could see the mountain stream where I used to go to get water for the shrine.

There was some light from within, so that I could see a cave. Earlier, I had caught glimpses of the cave many times, but not like this. Now, the cave wanted to enfold me in its arms.

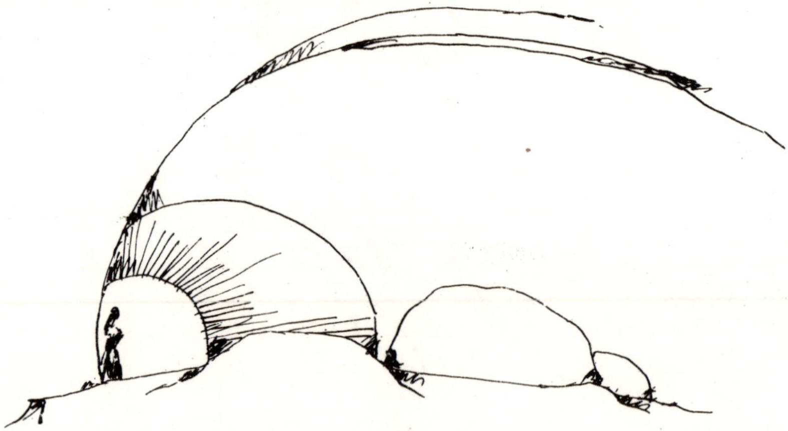

Cave Darshan (Vision)

The distance between one death and one birth —
I saw spread before my feet
and saw — that on the other side
there was a cave.
How far away it was — I didn't know...
at a distance of not one, but several deaths, perhaps.
But it felt...
as if it were calling back some memory.

Then the season of awareness changed —
the cave became lost in darkness...
and when the sharp wind of memory blew
It ruffled and scattered —
every black cloud of death.

Then once again on the other side
there appeared a cave.

God only knows at which instant
and through which Pir's grace it was
that I passed through the darkness of every death.

and reached the mouth of that cave...
The leaves of the wilderness ran towards me
and greeted me like long lost friends.
A spring took a handful of water
and sprinkled it on my forehead
An awakening took form and
led me by the hand into the cave...

If worship —
can be called passion
then I can tell you —
that cave was the shrine of my passion..
If a flat stone
can be called a marriage-bed
then I can tell you —
it was there that the five elements were wedded.

If the limbs of the body
are the flowers of worship
then I can tell you —
that the cave was filled with the fragrance of flowers.

I still can't remember
when I got back ...
And now —
I am standing, again,
at a distance from several deaths...

But this much I know —
that the thread of my awareness
passed through many deaths and entangles my being.
And even today
a part of this being
burns
like the diya, flame, of the shrine.

Shadow Pictures

There is a cave, I don't know where. Perhaps in some valley of Kashmir. Sometimes I glimpsed a fleeting shadow and sometimes I could see it clearly. This experience had been with me for many years; but in 1994, I had a cave vision in which there was a sense of timelessness. This cave, behind a waterfall, took me within its stone walls, and I saw some shadows of some past time like paintings on the walls.

Whatever I saw arose from out of my memories and appeared to be clinging to the walls. I realized that no word of it could come to my lips or in my writing. Feelingly I looked at the walls.

I wrote a poem — *Shadow Pictures*. But I know that only some of the experience is there, but to write more on that is not within my power.

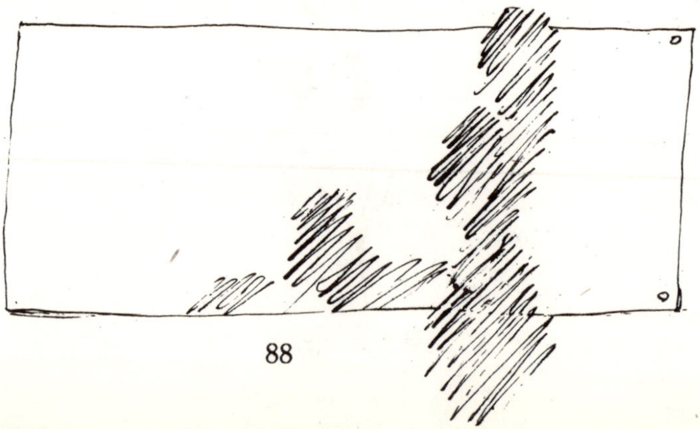

Shadow Pictures

That day when the sun
came to the mouth of the cave —
he came
wearing a royal robe of many colours.

God knows what it was within
that drew him to the cave
but the sun lowered his head
and crossed the threshold.
Inside — on the walls of that cave
he saw the shadow-pictures of kaya-yog,
figures intertwined in love
and sat down on a large stone...

The figures became breathing things, smiled
and began to speak, saying —
passing through the body,
whatever part of our being
crosses beyond —
that can never be pictured.

The rays of the sun blinked —
looked at the walls.
The stone —
became the seat of meditation
And the particles of energy from the very earth
within the cave
carried the sun beyond the pictures on the walls.

Then, when Time jarred the sun awake
the unearthly became earthly.
And seated on that same stone
the sun, taking the royal robe from his body
dressed himself in the walls of the cave...

I don't know —
in which era it happened
But this much I know — that there was a time once
when, looking at the shadow-pictures
on the walls of that cave,
the sun became a Dervish.

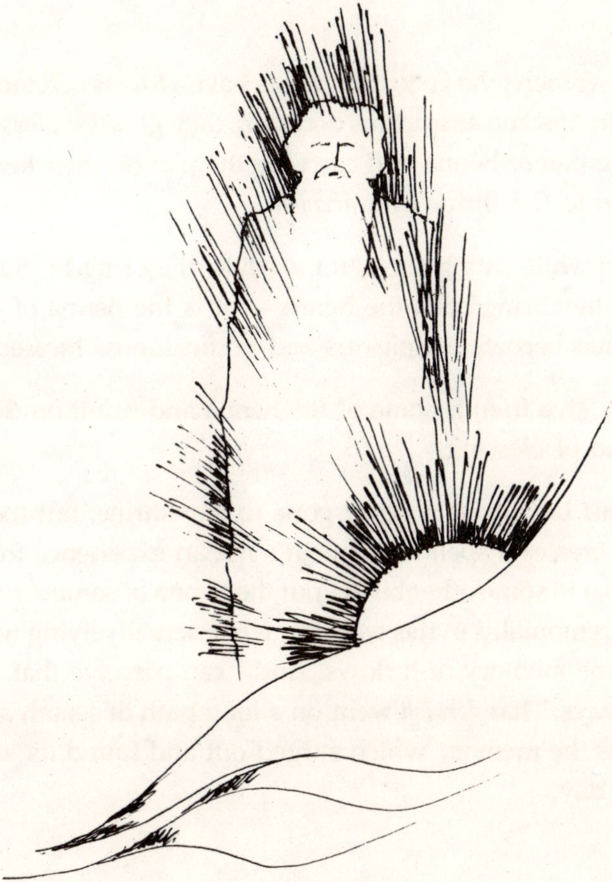

The Henna Of The Dervish

The women who go to the shrines have a lovely ceremony where before the start of some auspicious occasion, they go to be blessed. They prepare a large pan of henna and carrying the pan on their heads and singing, they go to the shrine of a *dervish*.

Even while sitting there, for a while, they sing in praise of god. And when they bring back the henna — it is the henna of the *dervish* which then has become auspicious and is considered blessed.

They give friends some of the henna and put it on their own hands as a kind of blessing.

In this birth I have never gone to any shrine, but there is a memory which creates a spell over me; it's not an experience from this birth. It seems that in some other birth I put the henna of some *dervish* on my hands. Not ceremonially, in this way. But while actually living with the *dervish*. Now some memory of it flows. And I can perceive that we went our separate ways. That *dervish* went on a long path of search and meditation. This was the memory which surged out and found its way into my words one day.

The Lila Of The Bathing Ghat

I knew that he,
passing through the lila of the eternal seed
had to go beyond

He said:
　　　　I had to cross the river
　　　　turning my body into a boat

but he found
there was no dock along the bank

Who knows
in which era this occurred
but when I made a dock of my body
this tale began

He tied the boat up to the dock
and said:
　　　　The rishis who call this dock
　　　　a place of pilgrimage
　　　　are telling the truth.
And that day he came to bathe

at this place of pilgrimage
This was our sacred bath
— mine and his
which brought such power
to my body
that I became the bathing ghat
on this side of the river,
and even on the other side.

He tied the boat of his body
to the ghat on the other side
and went in search
of the eternal seed

But he never came back.

I don't know from which era,
I am watching this lila of the bathing ghat, but

Sometimes, I tell this tale to the river.

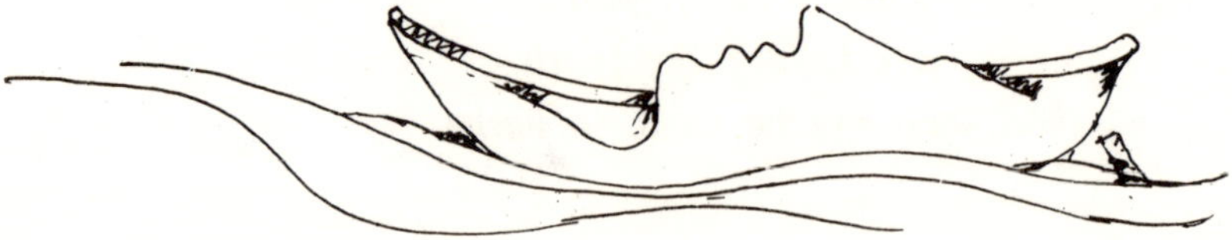

Meeting The Sky

Very often dreams are expressed in poems. But once, I wrote a poem and felt it was opening the door to some dream.

One day in the late afternoon, darkening the room a bit, I closed my eyes and said longingly, "Sai, I want to see you."

I don't know how much time passed before I saw a white light all around which I watched for some time. Then, I felt the whole sky darken with black clouds.

"Sai, you must be there, show yourself in this darkness."

I saw the red glow along the edge of the sky become dark. While I watched, it became redder and denser. I felt that that day Sai wanted to appear in the form of red light. The poem was *Embracing the Sky*.

Embracing The Sky

I wanted to meet the sky —for a while
but I stood around worrying
how to make my way through the mob of clouds...

Some clouds were jet black
God knows — from what time or which tradition...
Some of the clouds were thundering
as if they were Fate — the fate of travellers.

Some of the clouds were hissing in anger
like threats rising from rubble and ruins.
Some of the clouds were rising and falling
like the tattered leaves of ancestors.

Some were massing and staring —
They wanted to hold the whole sky in their fists,
wanted whoever passed their way
to cower by like a slave.

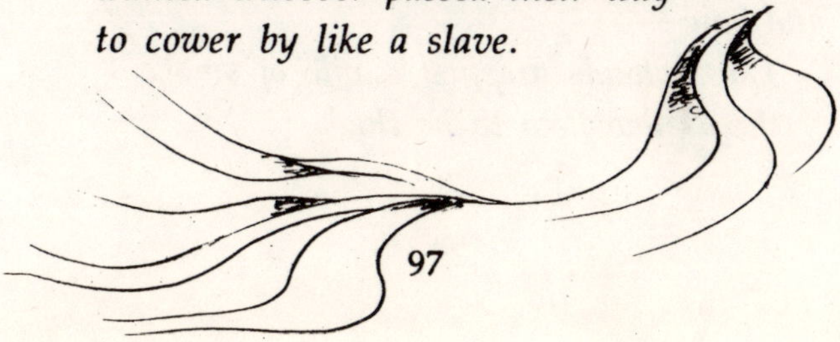

I didn't know who to say this to —
That there is a sky
within your very being
and it is the love of that
which makes it crave the heavens of the universe.

The worry about the mob of clouds
was not the worry of this small sky, but my own.
But it had had a taste of passion
and like a Dervish, crouched there
by the fire of my breath

Sitting at its side, I shared that fire
Said — this is between you and me
But when this passion wakes
the mob of clouds will hear of this.
So tell me, my Dervish
What will become of me?

It laughed — an unearthly blue laugh
and said —
These clouds are just a pile of smoke
they know how to be thick

and they know how to thunder too
and they tell you not to look at them,
but their frowns don't spring from the stars
and can't leave even a scratch on the body of the
blue sky

Again I said —

Taking you within me
how can I make my way
through this mob of clouds?
How can I ask these clouds, contorted with anger
to clear a path?

God knows what intense longing it had.
It watched me like a streak of lightning
and said —

You never ask anyone the way,
you don't even ask for a shoulder to cry on.
Don't be afraid and don't be taken in
and you'll pass right through the clouds
like the wind.

Five Dreams

One It was the night of January 30th, 1994 when I dreamt of a mountain valley, and there was a place where in the structures, you could see many paintings. When Imroz and I had seen those paintings, we went outside and saw a glorious profusion of the beauty of nature. Enormous flowers, red and white, were in bloom. There was a light shower, and all the flowers had become moist and had turned their faces to the sky. I said to Imroz, "No beauty could be more than this." I too felt like getting wet.

Two It was almost morning on the 8th of February, 1994 when I saw Sai standing near me. I quickly spread a sheet so he could sit down, but then I saw he was no longer there. So I went searching for him since he had just been there. Where had he gone?

Three On the night of the 18th of March, I dreamt that Sai was sitting in the corner by the side of my bed, where I actually keep his picture. Many candles were burning near a small place where I sometimes put flowers in front of his picture.

Four It was on the night of the 20th of March, when I dreamt I saw a peacock dancing, and I could see that on each and every feather was a picture. Some picture were of Hans Baba Devraha, some were of Rajneesh, and some of Sai.

Five Then, after two days, on the night of the 22nd, I dreamt that my right hand was closed in a fist, and when I opened it, I saw that there were many pictures on my palm, and there were many *rishis'* pictures on my fingertips. Astonished by it, I looked at my hand and then I heard the sound of some *mantra* coming from the hand. Then I saw that the *Śri Yantra* was written on my whole palm.

All these things that I had seen in dreams were so wonderful that they cast a spell on me. Almost a year passed before I wrote the poem, *Salute*, which carried the effect of these dreams.

Salute

Sometimes death too —
writes a book.
Then comes to Life —
and asks it to write the Foreword.

When she passed by the Bodhi tree —
watching, waiting for Buddha to open his eyes,
she trembled like a leaf on a tree.
She placed a sheet of wind before him
and Buddha told the tale of karuna, of compassion.

When she heard Krishna's flute,
she stood behind a tree
watching the raslila of the gopis
and trembled like a dancer's ankle bells.
Then making her way through a field of arms and corpses,
she held the reins of the chariot.
And when she placed the sheet of the wind before him,

Krishna smiled and recited the Gita.
Once, she went into the river Vei
and bathed the feet of Nanak for three days.
Then, sitting on the bank of the stream
she placed the sheet of the wind before him.
Nanak, filled with ecstasy, uttered Japji.

Death has several black books,
but there are several Forewords
like the light of the sun or moon
and for us mortals made of the dust of the earth —
these are our riches.

And then there was Sai Raju
who kept telling us, the bereft, of these riches.
*As for the serpents of wealth *—*
he washed his hands of them.
And wiping away the dust of time
he gave away those pearls with both hands.

** Serpents of wealth: In mythology, the riches of the dead go into the keeping of serpents.*

Death laughed —

No one reads my books or understands
People just set them aside
or tear out the Forewords
and lock them away as their own.
They become the serpents of wealth.

She said —

Who knows how Osho came to the world
but I have conversed with him.
Today, I have come to salute him.

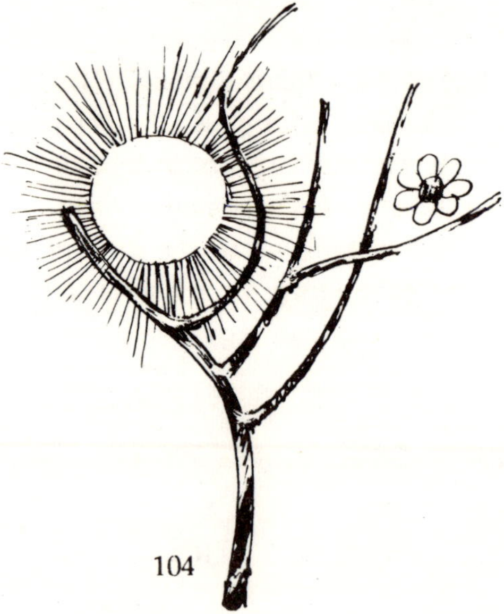

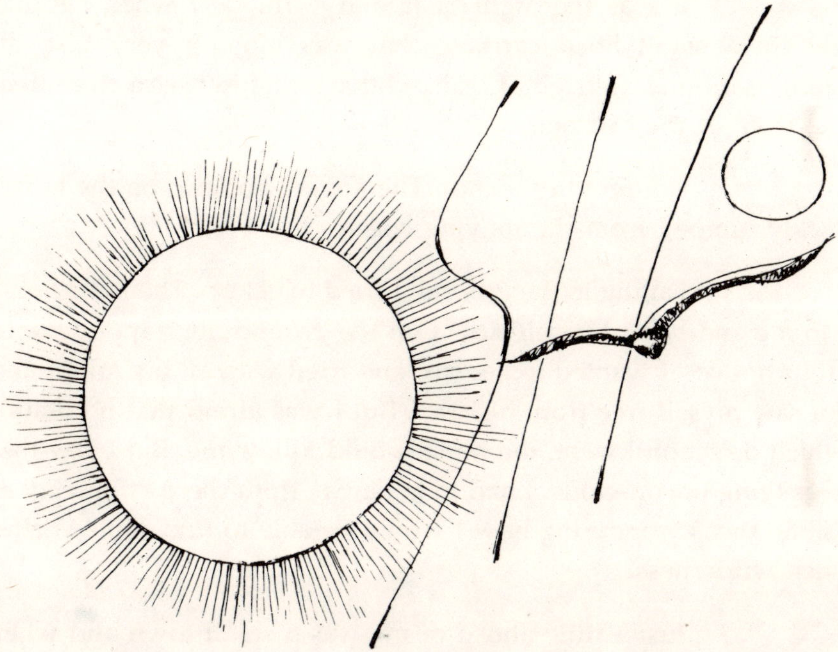

One Incident

It was the night of January 4th, 1991 when I found myself in a small horse-carriage that was moving very fast, all wilderness around. In fright, I realized that I couldn't see a coachman in the front of the carriage.

I caught my breath. There were no reins on the horse. I quickly jumped from the moving coach.

Falling to the ground, I tried to get up. Then, the horse ran to me and lying himself down on the ground, he trapped me in his four hooves. I wanted to get free and tried with all my might and again saw myself free from his trap. But I was afraid that no matter in which direction I went, the horse would follow me. But I saw that he was lying unconscious. I had to get away from there as quickly as possible. I was wondering how I would be able to find some shelter in such wilderness.

Just a little ahead of me was a small town and when I reached there, I saw that the whole town was asleep. No door was open and there was no light anywhere.

Then, walking through a narrow lane, suddenly I knocked at the door of a house. Till today, I don't know why I chose that particular house, but someone opened the door. The person who opened the door looked at me in surprise, and said — "Is this a dream?"

"I'm afraid it's not a dream."

"You've really come? We are meeting after so many births."

Who he was, I didn't know. I didn't recognize him, but I had a sense of relief. And I realized that I really was meeting him after many births.

This was a dream that haunted me, and whenever I remembered it, for a few moments I felt disoriented. I could see myself, still standing on the threshold of that house looking at the man who had opened the door.

I had never seen such a graceful and calm face. But who was he? In which birth had I met him? I was wrapped in the threads of this astonishment; four years passed.

Then, on the night of March 26th, 1995 I dreamt he was talking to me and I was able to write down this vision in a poem

The Door

A lonely road in the wilderness
a small carriage —
moving like the wind
I sat in it alone.
Afraid, the horse was galloping
there were no reins,
no coachman.
In that moment of terror I shuddered
and jumped from the coach.

A lonely road in the wilderness
I thought if there were earth beneath my feet
I'd find the way.
But the coach had stopped, stood still
and the horse, fuming with rage,
came and blocked my way.

I fell upon the ground.
He also fell

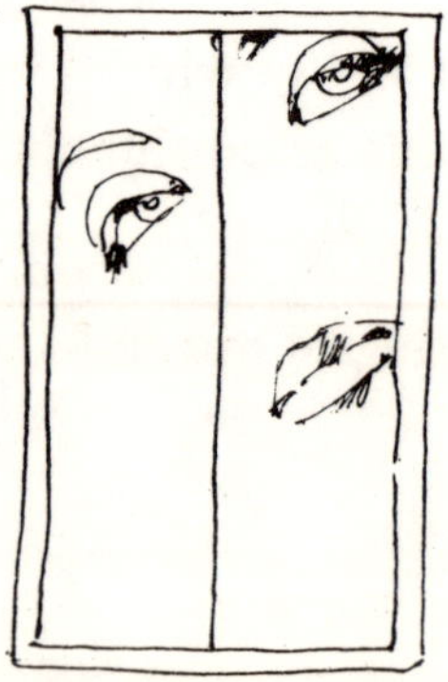

tangling me in his hooves
This was a time of doom
but what power entered me
like a streak of fire?
I freed myself from his trap.
He lay on the ground, thrashing his head
from side to side,
shuddering,
gasping for breath.

Dusk was falling.
I wandered on, glancing behind
afraid he was following me.
but no, I'd come quite far.
I don't know how far I walked
Then saw a bustee —
a bustee of sleeping houses.
Only I and the coming night.
No human being, not even a shadow of a human being
closed doors everywhere.
I went into a street
and who knows what struck me
but I stopped before a house and knocked at the door

I don't know who it was opened the door and said—
Have you really come? After many births?
I looked at him in amazement
didn't recognize him, but felt —
God's shadow
come to earth
I had no answer to the secret
but a peace descended over my entire body.

I said—
You don't know by which path I've come.
He smiled and said —
I know.
I asked —
If you know, where were you?
—very much there
—when...
I asked you to jump from the
reinless coach
released you from the horse's grip
showed you the way in the dark
and then stopped you
at this very door.
The door to your own home.

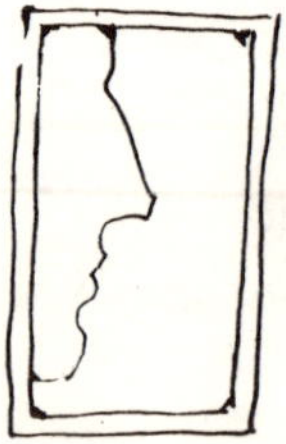

Visiting The Mound Of Death

Some information came to me from somewhere or other like a bat fluttering back and forth on the walls of the room. It is said that bats aim for the ears. That the darkness within the ears of a person attracts them as a place to hide. Therefore, the ears must be kept safe from bats. I felt all the flying rumours were like that — you had to keep your ears safe from them.

Only once, a few words came to my lips; again, this time? And I remembered Rajneesh who recognized the person who had come to assassinate him, but kept quiet. But when the man's mind changed, he was initiated by Rajneesh and then he himself told him why he had come.

The whole time, Rajneesh said: "Again, this time?"

The man didn't understand. But Rajneesh knew that this was the same man who had murdered him in the last life.

I felt that the same incident was being repeated in my life. I didn't say anything to anyone. Only Imroz knew that the person who had managed to have me killed in my last birth was thinking the same thing in this birth.

I thought that the meaning of life is to witness the wonder of love, not to breathe the poisonous air of violence and death.

This was the perception — that before this birth I had gone to the mound of death to find *kaya-yog*, begging for a wish to live for a while. And then to give Her (Death) the secret of life as an offering. Every bit of the whole poem, *Being and Becoming* represents the experience which I lived within.

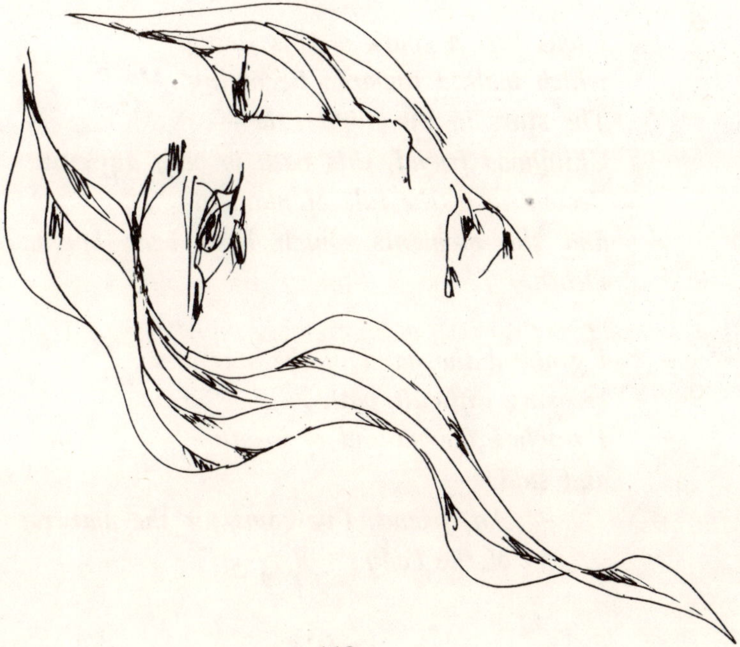

Being And Becoming

The lake of Being was cold and calm
A ray of sunshine came and
played a game of colours in the still waters
and I, with the ecstasy of these colours
began the journey of Becoming.

I was just a spark of this Being
which walked towards Becoming
The stars in the night said —
Childhood friend, this path is very difficult
Becoming is the tale of moments
and the moments which have been borrowed from Death.

I grabbed the hand of the star and
crossing difficult paths,
I reached the mound of Death
and said:
Ali, friend, I've come for the mantras
of the body.

Surprised, Death said:
How did you get here?
Don't you know none of my mantras works
on Being.
I answered:
Yes, friend, I know this.
Today, from this your place I've come to
take the yoga of the body.
From Being I want to Become.

Death laughed —
The people who want to leave their bodies
come to this mound of mine.
I read out the mantras of detachment
and piercing their earlobes
give them skulls as begging bowls.
but you...

And astonished, Death gave me the form of a body
and I received the mantras of breath

Then she showed me my reflection in the water
and said —
What will you do with your youth?
Go in the world of mortals
and you will die a death out of time.

I touched her feet, and said —
I have come, empty-handed
When I return from the land of the short-lived
I will surely bring an offering.

And having taken the form of a body I came to the world.
My every breath became a prayer
and who knows what this body was telling me —
Then, one day, it was your body
wearing the seven rays of the sun that came to me.
And then it played in my body
and I came to know a secret —
that this was the lila of love.

Neither a yogi
nor a worldly man knows

The seed is in Being
but blooms in Becoming.

The form of the body became meaningful
I went to the mound of Death to return to Being
again
and I paid her my homage
And the secret I had learned
I offered up to Death.

10 May, 1995

***Kama-yog**. Action/life on earth is important in order to advance spiritually through suffering*

The Sound Of Mantras

These were the last days of 1994. One night someone came in to my room and said: "The twenty-eighth *Lama* has come to meet you." I said: "All right, have him sit in the next room." And I quickly combed my hair. Then, I saw the hair on my head had become matted. In the dream I was upset when I saw my hair, but somehow I calmed down a bit. And thinking, who could this twenty-eighth *Lama* be, I went into the other room and saw that about 15-20 people were sitting there. I didn't know what was going on or who the *Lama* was; they were all dressed in white. Seeing all of them, I paid them homage and greeted them. Then, one of them, tall and thin, who was sitting there, got up and acknowledging my greeting, came to me and began to recite some *mantras* in my left ear. I woke with the sound of those *mantras* in my ears, but saw there was no one in the room.

Morning came and I remembered that somewhere in a book I had read that if someone recites a *mantra* in the left ear in a dream, it is an indication that you are to leave your body.

This mysterious occurrence hovered over me for many days and after about five months I wrote a poem — *Nadi da pattan* (Dock on the River).

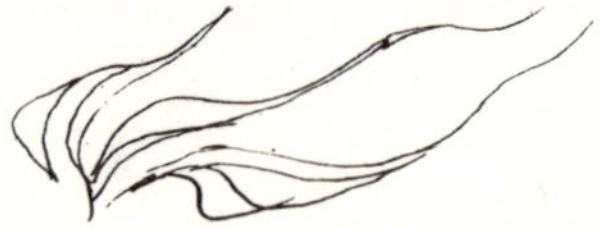

Dock On The River

I am standing on the dock of my consciousness
I don't know from what era
or on which mountain it was
that the stream of questions flowed
rushing through the valley
breaking the shoulders of the river.
And in the night when the stars in the sky
played over her breast
then the stream swept them away.

Frightened, I close my eyes
and the waves rise and drench even my dreams
When I wake,
I wring out my dreams
but can't understand a thing.
Only shiver to the depths of my body

Sai, standing on the dock
I've lived out many lives
but now, can stand here no longer

They say you are the khizar of the waters
So, my khizar, you must know what to do
But today, I will step into the stream,
and must cross beyond
the stream of questions.

24th May, 1995

Khizar : a deity of the water